WHEN I
FEEL ANGRY

WHEN I FEEL ANGRY

An Hachette UK Company
www.hachette.co.uk

Vie Books, an imprint of Summersdale Publishers
Part of Octopus Publishing Group Limited
Carmelite House
50 Victoria Embankment
LONDON
EC4Y 0DZ
UK

www.summersdale.com

This FSC® label means that materials used for the product have been responsibly sourced

MIX
Paper | Supporting responsible forestry
FSC® C018236

The authorised representative in the EEA is Hachette Ireland, 8 Castlecourt Centre, Castleknock Road, Castleknock, Dublin 15, D15 YF6A, Ireland

Printed and bound in Poland

ISBN: 978-1-80007-690-7

Substantial discounts on bulk quantities of Summersdale books are available to corporations, professional associations and other organizations. For details contact general enquiries: telephone: +44 (0) 1243 771107 or email: enquiries@summersdale.com.

WHEN I
FEEL ANGRY

A Child's Guide to Understanding and Managing Moods

Poppy O'Neill

CONTENTS

FOREWORD

Amanda Ashman-Wymbs
Counsellor and Psychotherapist, registered and accredited by
the British Association for Counselling and Psychotherapy

Anger is a difficult emotion for anyone to learn to cope with, and when our children are experiencing angry feelings, it can be hard to know where to begin to support them. This little workbook by Poppy O'Neill is a really useful place to start.

I have worked in the public and private sector with children for many years and brought up two daughters, and it is clear to me that we often need to help our children to understand anger and learn how to manage and process it.

This is a simple and fun workbook for children to use independently or with the support of their parents or carers. It is full of useful information and practices. Through fun exercises and activities, the child is taken on a journey of greater body awareness, as well as getting to know and understand their psychological, emotional and neurological processes in relation to anger and other big feelings.

The text is written in a very friendly and supportive style, normalizing the experience of being angry and encouraging the child to understand and feel confident in managing it. It covers vital areas such as how to calm the body and mind, how to manage anger at school, and how to increase emotional intelligence and vocabulary. It also helps the child to recognize the importance of having a healthy lifestyle and how to calm down and express anger in positive ways.

I highly recommend this much needed self-help book for supporting children in learning to understand and cope with anger and its related issues in a positive, fun and clear way.

INTRODUCTION: A GUIDE FOR PARENTS AND CARERS

When I Feel Angry is a practical guide for children to manage feelings of anger. Using activities and ideas based on therapeutic techniques developed by child psychologists, this book will help your child understand their emotions, express their anger in healthy ways and learn to calm themselves when they feel overwhelmed.

Anger is a normal, healthy emotion that all children – and adults – experience. As your child grows they'll encounter things that cause them to feel angry, but unless they develop the appropriate emotional intelligence it can become difficult to process that anger.

The most important thing to remember is that we don't need to be afraid of our children's anger. This isn't always simple, as it can be difficult to separate angry feelings from the sometimes destructive behaviours that come along with them. Turn to page 137 for more information and advice on how you can support your child to deal with anger in a healthier way.

We all struggle with anger on occasion – whether our feelings are rational or irrational – but sometimes children can become quick to anger, which can cause issues with school, friendships and at home. Sometimes, no matter how much you support them to cope with their big feelings, they struggle to control their anger. The truth is, dealing with anger doesn't mean never feeling it – it's about being more comfortable with feeling it and having strategies in place to express anger in a more positive way.

This book is aimed at children aged 7–11, a time when emotions can run high. School gets more serious, friendships can become more complex and the early stages of puberty mean changes in their body too. It's no wonder some children find it overwhelming to deal with all these new and somewhat daunting experiences. If this sounds like your child, you're not alone. With your support and understanding, it's possible for your child to build their emotional intelligence – bringing with it the confidence to navigate challenges, control their emotions and grow into a positive, respectful young person.

Signs your child might struggle to regulate their anger

Behaviours such as these are typical of children who struggle with anger:

- They never quite grew out of "tantrums"

- They find it difficult to accept change or disagreement

- They blame others for their problems

- They often need your help to calm down

- They find it difficult to compromise

If you recognize your child in this list, don't panic. It's important to remember that taking an interest in your child's emotional experiences can be a difficult step, but it's also an incredibly positive one. It's OK if you're not sure what to do or how to help your child. Learning to manage anger is about developing emotional intelligence over a lifetime; it isn't something that can be fixed or achieved quickly, which means it's never too late to start building it.

How to use this book: For parents and carers

This book is for your child, so how involved you'll be will depend on them. Some children might be happy working through the activities by themselves, while others might want or need a little guidance and encouragement.

Let your child know it's OK to ask for help and to set their own pace. Building emotional intelligence involves trusting in their abilities and allowing them to make their own decisions.

The activities are designed to get your child thinking about themselves and the way their mind and emotions work, helping them to cope with anger and express it in healthy ways.

Hopefully this book will be helpful for you and your child, fostering greater understanding of angry feelings and how to deal with them. However, if you have any serious concerns about your child's mental health, your GP is the best person to go to for further advice.

HOW TO USE THIS BOOK: A GUIDE FOR CHILDREN

Do you ever feel angry? Everybody feels angry sometimes. If your angry feelings ever feel too big – you're not alone. Angry feelings are difficult and it's very normal to find them challenging.

Sometimes, though, angry feelings can get in the way of being yourself and having fun. Here are some signs this might be happening for you:

 You sometimes find it difficult to play with other children

 Calming yourself is really hard

 You feel angry a lot of the time

 When you feel angry, you sometimes do things you wish you hadn't

If that sounds like you, you're not the only one! Lots of children feel this way, they just have different ways of showing it on the outside. This book is here to help you understand your angry feelings, get more comfortable with emotions and learn tricks for feeling calm.

There are lots of activities and ideas to help you learn all about anger, thoughts and emotions. You can go at your own pace and you can ask a trusted grown-up for help at any time. There might be things in the book that you'd like to chat about with your grown-up, too. This book is for you and the activities are about you – so you're the expert!

INTRODUCING
RAH THE MONSTER

Hi there! My name's Rah and I'm here to guide you through this book. Inside you'll find lots of interesting ideas and fun activities. Are you ready? Let's jump in!

PART 1:
ALL ABOUT YOU

In this chapter we'll learn all about you! Getting to know yourself, what makes anger bubble up inside you and how anger feels are important parts of understanding your emotions.

ACTIVITY: ALL ABOUT ME

First let's find out some facts about you.

My name is...

I am...   years old

My favourite fruit is...

My favourite thing
to play is...

I love to make...

My favourite colour is...

ACTIVITY: MY HOME

Now let's find out a little bit about where you live.

I live in a…

House   Bungalow

Castle   Flat   Boat

Treehouse   Caravan

From my window I can see…

Who lives with you in your home? Draw them here:

Draw your home here:

ACTIVITY: WHAT DOES ANGER FEEL LIKE?

Imagine you are feeling really angry. What happens to your body when you feel anger? Circle your answer, or write your own.

What happens to your face?

I scrunch it up

My bottom lip sticks out

I bite my teeth together

Something else:

Can you draw your angry face here?

What happens to your arms and legs?

 My hands make fists

 I want to run, jump or stamp my feet

 My muscles feel tense

 Something else:

What happens inside your body?

 My tummy feels tight

 My head aches

 My heart beats faster

 Something else:

When we're angry, we can feel it all over our bodies.

Anger feels different for everybody, because we're all unique!

I AM KIND TO MYSELF

ACTIVITY: WHAT MAKES ME FEEL ANGRY?

Everybody is different and the types of things that make us feel angry are different too.

Colour in yellow the things on this page that annoy you a bit.

Colour in red the things that make you feel angry.

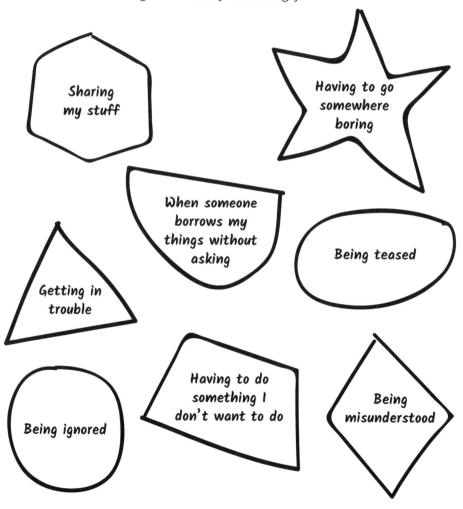

Sharing my stuff

Having to go somewhere boring

When someone borrows my things without asking

Being teased

Getting in trouble

Being ignored

Having to do something I don't want to do

Being misunderstood

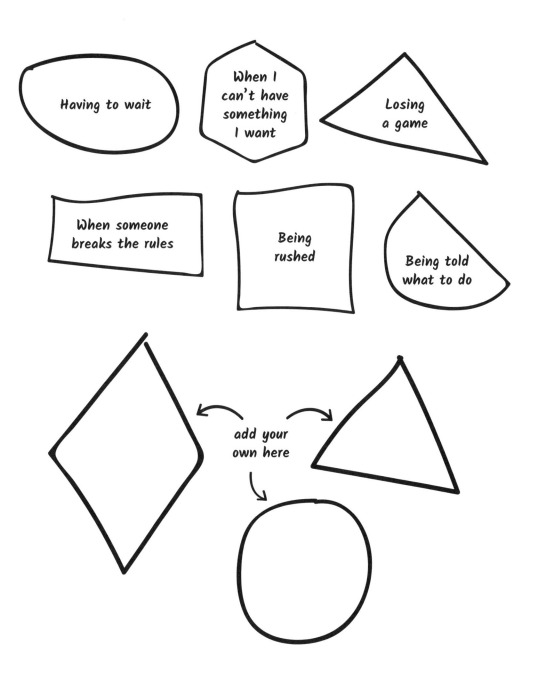

Having to wait

When I can't have something I want

Losing a game

When someone breaks the rules

Being rushed

Being told what to do

add your own here

ACTIVITY: TRUE OR FALSE?

How much do you know about anger? Circle true or false, then turn the book upside down to find out the answer!

1. I shouldn't feel angry

TRUE   FALSE

2. Anger is a bad emotion

TRUE   FALSE

3. Anger is all in your brain

TRUE   FALSE

4. If you ignore angry feelings, they go away

TRUE   FALSE

5. Anger is a helpful emotion

TRUE   FALSE

1. False – It's OK to feel any emotion, as long as you express it in a safe way

2. False – No emotions are bad! Anger can *feel* uncomfortable, because it's a signal that something doesn't feel right

3. False – Just like other emotions, anger is a mix of brain and body feelings

4. False – Emotions need to be let out by being expressed (see Part 4)

5. True – Anger helps us work out what's important to us and what we feel sensitive about

I BELIEVE
IN MYSELF

ACTIVITY: A TIME I FELT ANGRY

We all feel angry sometimes and the feeling of anger can get really big inside our bodies. Sometimes anger can lead us to do or say things that hurt other people or get us in trouble… things that we'd probably never do when we're feeling calm.

It's never OK to hurt people or damage things, but everyone makes mistakes sometimes, and we can always try to put things right and learn from them.

Can you think of a time you felt angry? Write or draw about it here:

Continue drawing about your feelings here:

PART 2: GETTING TO KNOW ANGRY FEELINGS

Feeling angry is a normal part of being human. Just like other emotions, it's great to get to know our angry feelings, because it helps us understand ourselves better and become more in control. In this chapter you'll learn all about how feelings work.

WHAT ARE EMOTIONS?

Emotions aren't something we can see or touch, or look at under a microscope. They are a way that our brain and body communicate. When our body's senses – sight, smell, touch, taste and hearing – pick up something that seems important, emotions show our brain how to respond.

Rah misses Pop – they haven't seen each other in a long time.

When Rah and Pop see each other again, Rah feels so happy!

Rah runs to greet Pop.

Emotions can also be caused by thoughts – if we think about a sad film or memory, we'll feel sad.

Everyone's emotions are different, because our lives have all been different. For example, if ginger cats remind you of a funny memory, you might feel happy when you see a ginger cat. But if a ginger cat once scratched you, you might feel worried when you see a ginger cat.

Why do we feel emotions?

Thousands of years ago, human beings evolved to feel emotions because they helped to keep them alive. For example, feeling fear of dangerous animals meant early humans knew to run away so they didn't get eaten.

Although dangers like this are now much less common, our emotions are still an important part of how we experience the world. They help to bring colour to our lives, experiences and relationships.

WHY DO WE FEEL ANGRY?

Anger is often a sign that something's happened that's not OK with you. Angry feelings can happen when we can't get what we want, or are told to do something we don't want to do. So, when we feel like we don't have enough control, anger can be a way our brain tries to get us more control.

Just because we feel angry, doesn't always mean anything is wrong. And just because someone is angry with you, doesn't always mean you've done something wrong. Sometimes, it just means we want different things to the people around us.

It's OK to feel angry, even if you're not really sure why you're feeling that way.

Anger is a tricky emotion because it can make us want to explode! When we feel angry, our body might want to fight or shout in a way it doesn't when we feel calm.

Hurting others or damaging things is never OK, even when we feel angry. It harms people and does not solve the problem that caused the angry feelings in the first place. Keep reading to find out more about angry feelings and how to let them out in ways that work for everybody.

Can you help Rah find his way out of the maze away from the exploding anger bomb and toward calm?

ALL EMOTIONS ARE OK

Every single person on Earth (and every astronaut in space) has emotions – even if they don't always show it on the outside.

When you remember that all emotions are OK, that none of them can harm you and that you are in charge of your actions, you unlock the superpower of resilience. Resilience means feeling your feelings and expressing them in ways that help you feel calm.

If you feel angry, that's OK – you can move your body, talk about your feelings and feel your anger. Just like all the other emotions, anger tells us what's important to us, what we like and don't like.

ACTIVITY:
HOW DO YOU FEEL RIGHT NOW?

Take a moment to close your eyes and think about how your body and mind feel right now. Write or draw about your feelings here – you could include any thoughts that are on your mind, too.

MY FEELINGS
MATTER

RAH FEELS ANGRY

Rah's after-school football club has been cancelled today and Rah feels angry about it.

When Rah feels angry, Rah's body feels…

 Hot

 Tense

 Full of energy

Rah's heart beats faster and it gets hard for Rah to think about anything other than the anger.

When Rah feels very angry, Rah wants to…

 Stamp

 Kick

 Shout

 Hit

 Scream

 Push

 Slam doors

 Throw things

 Use unkind words

Have you ever felt angry like Rah? Draw a circle around any of the actions you've taken or felt like taking when you're angry.

ACTIVITY: LEVELS OF ANGER

Sometimes we feel only a little bit angry and at other times our angry feelings are huge! It's useful to have lots of words so we can give a name to how we are feeling.

Scientists have discovered that naming our emotions helps us feel calmer and more in control. It also helps those around us to understand how we are feeling inside.

Here are some words we use for different levels of anger:

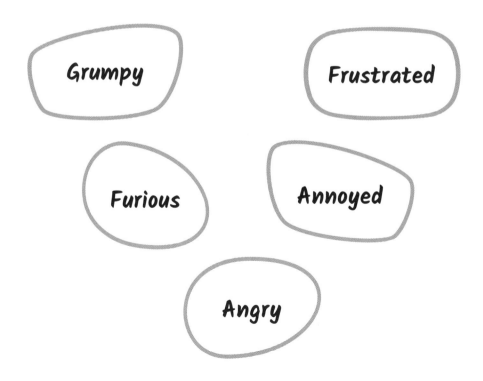

Can you put the words below in order, from smallest feeling to biggest? Write the number you think each emotion is in the box, with 1 for smallest and 5 for biggest.

Grumpy

Annoyed

Frustrated

Angry

Furious

ACTIVITY: WORDSEARCH

There are lots of other ways to feel angry. Can you find them in the wordsearch?

I	R	R	I	T	A	T	E	D	I
W	E	E	R	T	I	Y	U	O	M
P	A	S	S	D	F	G	H	J	P
K	L	E	F	U	M	I	N	G	A
Z	C	N	V	B	N	M	I	X	T
O	U	T	R	A	G	E	D	R	I
H	L	F	V	N	A	S	T	H	E
B	V	U	D	E	W	M	H	A	N
Y	R	L	I	V	I	D	U	P	T
A	S	G	B	O	X	K	D	O	M

Irritated	Resentful	Fuming
Outraged	Impatient	Livid

Are any of these words new to you? If so, you can use a dictionary to learn more about their meanings. The more words you have for your feelings, the better!

ACTIVITY:
ANGER IS LIKE A VOLCANO

Lava forms under the Earth's crust, just like angry feelings begin inside your body and mind. When emotions are red-hot like lava, they get difficult to control and we end up behaving in ways we wish we hadn't. Taking action to calm your body cools red-hot emotions before they erupt!

Colour in the volcano – you can use pens, pencils, crayons, paint, collage… whatever you have nearby. See Part 3 for ways to feel calm.

I CAN STAND UP FOR MYSELF

ACTIVITY: MAKE YOUR OWN VOLCANO

Ask a grown-up to help you with this fun science activity. You'll see the "lava" erupt just like big, angry feelings. This experiment is best done outdoors or in the bath so it doesn't make too much mess!

You will need:

 Sand or old towels

 A 2-litre plastic bottle

 Funnel

 1 tbsp bicarbonate of soda

 2 cups white vinegar

 Red or orange food colouring (optional)

How to:

1. Prop up the bottle in a mound of sand or with old towels.

2. Use your funnel to pour the bicarbonate of soda into the bottle.

3. Add the food colouring (if using) to the vinegar, then pour the mixture into the bottle – watch it erupt!

HOW ANGER MAKES US BEHAVE

We learned about some of the things our body wants to do when we feel angry on page 19. Anything that hurts you or someone else, or damages things is an unhelpful behaviour. We call them unhelpful because they cause problems rather than solve them.

When we feel very angry, the part of our brain that can think clearly – called the pre-frontal cortex, which is in charge of our mind when we're calm – isn't in charge. The part of our brain that's responsible for emotions – the amygdala – is in charge instead. This often means we make choices and behave in ways that are all about our anger, and not about keeping ourselves safe and being kind to ourselves and others.

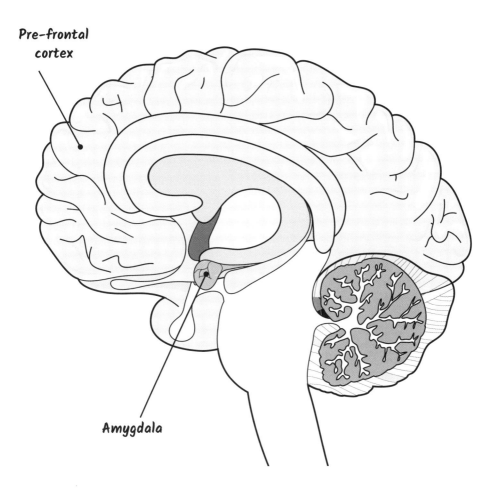

Pre-frontal
cortex

Amygdala

WHEN SOMEONE ELSE IS ANGRY

How does it feel when you're around someone who is showing big, angry feelings? For most people, it can feel quite scary, especially if that person is angry with you. It's OK for other people to feel anger, as long as they do not hurt you, themselves or others, or damage things. But if someone is behaving in a way that frightens you, it's OK to ask for help from a trusted grown-up, or to get away from them.

On the other hand, if someone is angry and they're expressing their angry feelings in a respectful way, they're not doing anything wrong. We're all allowed to stand up for ourselves when we're angry! For advice on how to express anger in healthy ways, see Part 4.

I AM
BRAVE

PART 3:
HOW TO FEEL CALM

It's hard to think clearly when you feel very angry. That's why calming your body is an important skill to learn. When your body feels calm, you're able to make good choices and be kind to yourself and others. In this chapter we'll find out about lots of different ways to feel calm.

NAMING YOUR EMOTIONS

Remember learning about different words for different types of anger on page 39? Using words to describe your feelings is a brilliant way to help yourself feel calm. As you identify your emotions, you feel calm because you have become aware of them.

You can do it any time. Try it now!

1. Close your eyes and put your hand on your chest.

2. Take a deep breath in, and out.

3. Think about how you feel.

4. Say, out loud, what you are feeling.

I feel angry

If you practise naming your feelings while you're calm, it will be easier to remember to try it when you feel big emotions like anger, fear or excitement, too. Naming your emotions makes you feel a little calmer because it reminds you that feelings are just feelings and they don't last forever.

ACTIVITY: MINDFUL FEET

Practising mindfulness often means focusing all your attention on what is happening right now. When you're feeling a big emotion, or having a hard time, you can use mindfulness to help your mind and body feel calm.

Try this mindful activity:

 Feel the bottoms of your feet.

 What temperature can you feel? Are some parts of your feet warmer or cooler than others?

 What textures can you feel with your feet? Perhaps soft socks or gritty sand?

 Can you move your toes one by one? Are some more difficult to move on their own than others?

 Use the feet templates to draw or write what you can feel. You can use patterns, words, pictures or diagrams – you choose!

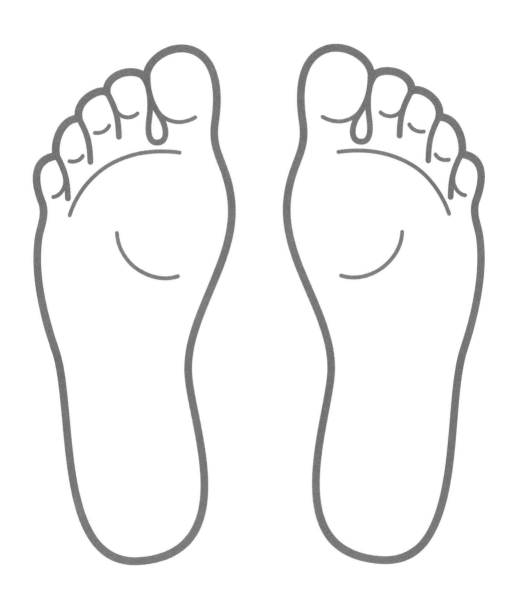

ACTIVITY: PEACEFUL BELLY BREATHING

Taking a really deep breath is an instant calmer-downer. Belly breathing delivers oxygen to every part of your body, plus it helps you relax and let go of big emotions and worries.

Here's a fun way to learn belly breathing:

 Grab a teddy and lie on your back.

 Put the teddy on your belly.

 Take a deep breath in through your nose, and see if you can lift up the teddy by sending your in-breath down into your belly – no hands allowed.

 Now let the air slowly out through your nose. Try not to let the teddy fall.

What else could you lift with your belly breaths?

A slipper?

A cookie?

This book?

What could Rah lift up with a really deep breath? Use your imagination to draw something for Rah to lift.

ACTIVITY: TIGER VISUALIZATION

Visualization is a way of relaxing your body and your mind at the same time. Read this meditation to yourself and then imagine it, or ask a grown-up to read it to you.

Close your eyes and take three deep breaths in and out through your nose. You can relax and just be. Now, imagine a tiger – this tiger represents your angry feelings. The tiger belongs to you and cannot hurt you. You are in charge of caring for the tiger, you have trained the tiger to do as you say, and you and your tiger can talk to each other. What kind of home does your tiger live in? Picture the tiger and its home.

Can you think of a time recently when you felt frustrated, angry or even furious? Remember how you felt and now think of your tiger as those angry feelings. Is your tiger big or small? Is your tiger growling, showing its teeth? Is it moving or staying still?

Now, imagine asking your angry tiger what it needs to help it feel calm. Perhaps your tiger needs a hug, or to know that you're OK. Perhaps your tiger wants to speak and be listened to. Stay still for a moment and see what your tiger says. Once you know what your tiger needs, you can imagine giving your tiger all it needs to feel safe and calm. How's your tiger doing now? Feeling calm, perhaps even a bit sleepy? You're doing a great job.

When your tiger is lovely and calm and ready for a nap, imagine stroking its warm, soft fur and saying "goodnight".

Take another deep breath in and out through your nose, and open your eyes when you're ready.

This is a lovely visualization to do whenever you're having trouble letting angry feelings out, or you have an experience or memory that's bothering and annoying you.

Can you draw your tiger here?

I AM
IN CONTROL

TALK ABOUT YOUR FEELINGS

Talking about how you're feeling is a brilliant habit to get into. Sharing our emotions is how we get to know each other. When you feel angry, using words to express how you feel inside helps you feel calmer.

Here are some useful phrases for talking about angry feelings:

It's not just anger that needs to be talked about – you can talk about any feelings, even when you don't really know what to call them.

WHO CAN I TALK TO?

Talking about feelings is normal and you can do it any time. But when emotions get really big, you're having trouble getting calm or you're feeling angry so often that it's getting in the way of feeling good, it's time to talk to a trusted grown-up. If there's something unfair that's happened to you, that's made you feel very angry, that's also something to tell a trusted grown-up.

A trusted grown-up could be your parent, carer, relative, family friend, teacher or someone else who works at your school. You'll know they're a trusted grown-up because you feel safe and calm around them.

Can I talk to you about something?

Who could you talk to? Write or draw about your trusted grown-up or grown-ups here:

If you can think of one person, that's plenty!

MOVE YOUR BODY

We feel emotions like anger all over our bodies. This is because of our nervous system – a complicated web of connections that links the brain to every part of the body.

When you feel angry, your brain releases chemicals that give you a burst of energy, and your nervous system is activated, making you feel tense and hot.

Movement is an easy way to let that tension out of your body. There are lots of ways to move! Here are just a few:

Running
Running on the spot or around your garden

Dancing
Shake and wiggle your body however feels good!

Drumming
Use your knees or a pillow to beat a rhythm

Jumping

Jump on the spot or
on a trampoline

Humming

Humming or singing creates
vibrations and movement
inside your body

Stretching

Stretch your arms and legs
to relax your muscles

Moving your body calms your emotions because it sends calming vibrations
from your body to your nervous system and brain.

ACTIVITY: MY CALM PLACE

Your calm place is somewhere you can imagine being in when you want to feel calm. It can be anywhere you feel safe, relaxed and comfortable. It might be somewhere you know well, or somewhere you've invented using your imagination!

Rah's calm place is in the countryside, by a gentle stream of water.

Think about where your calm place could be – can you draw it here?

Imagine being in your calm place right now. What sounds can you hear?

_____

_____

_____

What can you smell?

_____

_____

_____

What's special about your calm place?

_____

_____

_____

ACTIVITY: THE 5-4-3-2-1 TRICK

Here's a great way to feel calm that you can use wherever you happen to be. It uses mindfulness practices to redirect your attention from big emotions and help you keep your cool.

Sit quietly and notice:

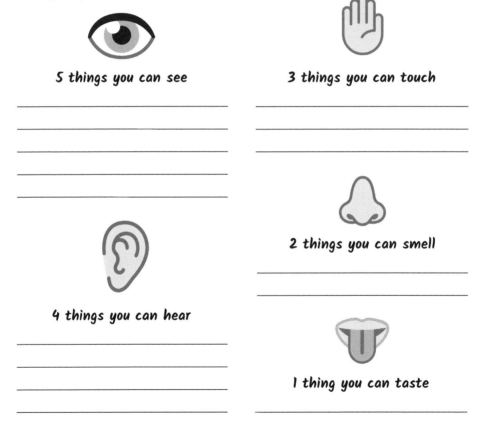

5 things you can see

_____

_____

_____

_____

3 things you can touch

_____

_____

_____

2 things you can smell

_____

_____

4 things you can hear

_____

_____

_____

_____

1 thing you can taste

_____

You don't need to write them down, say them out loud or remember them – just noticing is enough. You can do this trick as many times as you need to – there's always something for our senses to notice!

FEELING CALM AT SCHOOL

There are all sorts of things that can make you feel angry during the school day. Other children, lessons that you don't enjoy and changes to the routine to name just a few.

Having to sit at a desk can make it extra difficult to let angry feelings out, so here are some ideas for keeping calm at school:

Make sure you move your body at break times	Put your hand up and talk to your teacher if something is wrong	Ask for help if you feel really angry
Count to ten	Use the 5-4-3-2-1 trick (page 66)	Think about your calm place (page 64)
Use your fingers to tap quietly on your knees	Place your hand on your belly for sitting-up belly breaths (page 54)	Name your feelings (page 51)

What makes you feel angry during school time? Write or draw about it here:

I CAN TAKE A DEEP BREATH

PART 4: EXPRESSING ANGER IN HEALTHY WAYS

Just like other emotions, when anger builds inside us, it's important to let it out! What makes anger tricky is that letting it out safely can be more difficult. In this chapter we'll learn lots of ways to let anger out so that it doesn't harm you or others.

ACTIVITY: PRESSING PAUSE

Pressing pause lets us stop and think before we act. It's hard to press pause on our actions when we're feeling big emotions, but with practice, it gets easier. You can practise pressing pause any time. Here's how to do it:

 Imagine you have a remote control that has power over your emotions.

 When you feel an emotion building, you can press pause so you have a moment to think before you express your emotions.

 When your emotions are paused, you can choose how you express them in ways that don't hurt yourself or others. You can take a deep breath and make a good choice.

 You can press play when you're ready to express yourself in a safe way.

Colour in the remote control and add numbers and symbols to the buttons. If you could give your remote control other powers, what would they be?

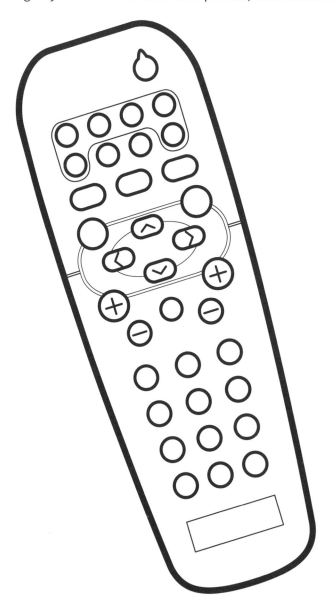

ACTIVITY: SCRIBBLE IT OUT!

You can use pens and pencils to express your anger. Pressing down on the paper and letting your pen or pencil move quickly and freely will help let angry feelings out of your body.

These pages are especially for you to scribble all over – go for it!

Add more scribbles here!

ACTIVITY: WRITE ABOUT YOUR FEELINGS

When we feel angry, we sometimes want to say things to others that will hurt their feelings or frighten them. Even if it feels pretty satisfying while you're full of anger, it doesn't feel good for long and it can hurt friendships when you act in this way.

Another way to let these unkind, angry words out is to write them down. Once they're written down, you can rip or scrunch the paper, and throw them away. Ripping and scrunching paper feels good when you're angry too!

Use this space to write down angry words and thoughts. When you're ready, you can tear out the page, scrunch and tear it up, and throw it in the recycling.

_____

_____

_____

_____

_____

_____

_____

_____

_____

_____

_____

_____

_____

_____

ACTIVITY: PUSHBACK

Pushback is a brilliant game that you can play with a trusted grown-up when you feel angry. It can help you feel calmer by letting the angry feelings move out of your body. Here's how to play:

 Face your grown-up and either link hands with them or press your palms together, like this:

 Your grown-up's job is to stay still and your job is to push against their hands, letting out your angry feelings through pushing.

 See if making a funny face or noises helps. This game is even better if you end up laughing!

This game is fun any time, so you don't have to save it only for when you're feeling angry.

ACTIVITY: GET CREATIVE

Being creative and using your imagination is how your mind plays. When you use angry feelings to create something new, your mind and body can relax and let some of the anger and tension out.

Use this space to draw your anger as a monster or animal. You could add stormy weather, a landscape and words to your drawing. Let your imagination guide you!

EVERYBODY FEELS ANGRY SOMETIMES

TAKING A BREAK

When anger feels really big in your body and you can't think straight, it's time to take a break. Sometimes moving away from the cause of your anger is enough to calm those feelings, and sometimes you'll need to use a calming trick or express your anger to let it out.

It can be difficult to ask for a break, especially when your mind is clouded with angry feelings. Using a hand signal could be an easier way to say that you need some space to calm down. Luckily, lots of people understand this hand signal to mean "time out":

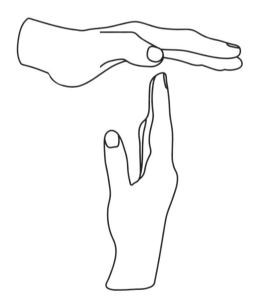

If your family, carers, teachers and friends don't know this one, it's easy to teach! Once you know it, you can use it to ask for a break when you need one.

DEALING WITH HUGE ANGRY FEELINGS

When you're feeling super angry and you've just got to let the feelings out, what can you do? Here are some things to do when you need to get the anger out in a hurry!

Rip up scrap paper
Scrunch it between your fingers!

Squidge playdough
Turn the page for a playdough recipe!

Do five wall push-ups
Pushing helps calm your body and brain

Wrap your arms around yourself and squeeze
A big, firm hug helps you feel safe and calm

Push your hands together, then let go
This helps relax your muscles

Stretch up high
This lets the tension out of your body

ACTIVITY:
HOW TO MAKE PLAYDOUGH

Playdough is soft and squidgy, which makes it great for letting angry feelings out of your body. It's not for eating, because it doesn't taste very nice. Use it to squish, rub, roll, splat and make into shapes! Here's how to make your own (but ask a grown-up before you start):

You will need:

 8 tbsp plain flour, plus extra for dusting

 2 tbsp table salt

 60 ml warm water

 1 tbsp vegetable oil

 Food colouring – follow packet instructions (optional)

How to:

1. Mix the flour and salt in a bowl. In another bowl, mix the water, oil and food colouring if you're using it.

2. Pour the water mixture into the flour mixture a little at a time and stir until the mixture forms a dough.

3. Use a little more flour to dust a work surface, and knead your mixture until it becomes smooth and soft. Your playdough is ready to play with!

4. Store in the fridge in an airtight bag or container.

RAH'S ANGRY WORDS

Rah is feeling ANGRY and wants to let it out. Instead of roaring loudly and scaring others, Rah uses words! Can you colour Rah's and the other monsters' words?

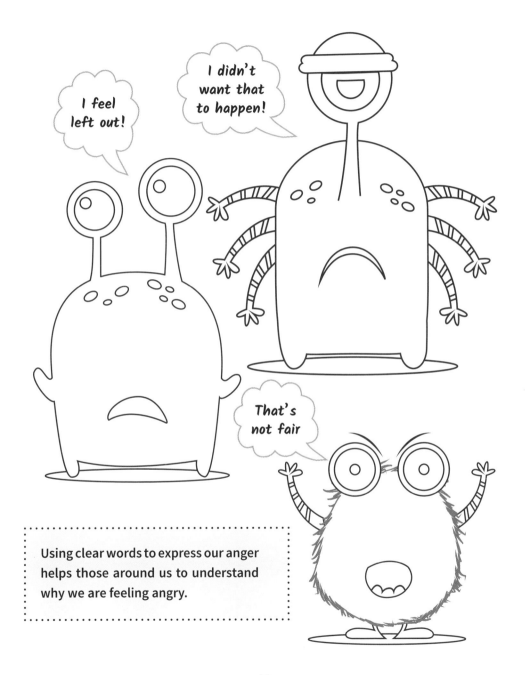

Using clear words to express our anger helps those around us to understand why we are feeling angry.

I AM
RESPECTFUL

ACTIVITY: ANGRY ANIMALS

Animals feel angry too, just like humans. Take a look at these animals – they're all feeling angry! What noise do they make? Join up the animals to their angry noises by drawing a line.

Squawk!

Woof!

Roar!

Hiss!

Grrr!

ACTIVITY: YOGA ANIMALS

We can take inspiration from these animals when we want to calm our own angry feelings, using yoga. Yoga is a way of stretching and moving your body to help you relax and feel good. Try these poses:

Lion

Sit on your knees, lean forward, open your mouth and let out a big, loud breath!

Cat

On your hands and knees, stretch your spine up to the ceiling.

Cow

On your hands and knees, drop your belly down and stick your bottom up to the ceiling.

Dog

Start on your hands and knees, then push your bottom up and back.

Eagle

Stand on one leg and twist the other leg around your standing leg. Twist your arms around each other.

ACTIVITY: MAKE ANGER FLASHCARDS

When you feel really angry it can be hard to think of safe ways to express anger or calm your body. Flashcards like these will help you remember your anger skills when it's difficult. Sometimes it's difficult to speak calmly when you're feeling very angry. Flashcards are a good way to show the people around you how they can help.

On one side of each flashcard you'll find an idea for how to calm angry feelings. On the other, you'll find a message to show a trusted grown-up.

Colour and carefully cut out the flashcards, and keep them somewhere you can find them in a hurry.

I can move my body	I can take a deep breath
I can draw an angry picture	I can take a break
I can ask for help	I can move away from what's making me feel angry

Can you take
a deep breath
with me?

I need to move
my body

I need to
take a break

Can you sit
with me while
I calm down?

Can I go
outside?

Can you help
me calm down?

ACTIVITY:
WHEN I FEEL ANGRY, I CAN...

Phew! We've learned so many different ways to deal with angry feelings. Which ones will you use next time you feel angry? Write or draw your top three skills you learned in this chapter:

PART 5:
TAKING GOOD CARE OF YOU

Taking care of your body and mind will help you feel your best and deal with whatever the day brings. In this chapter you'll learn all about why being kind to your body and mind makes you calm, strong and resilient.

WHY IS TAKING CARE OF YOUR BODY IMPORTANT?

Emotions happen in our body and mind, so the healthier and better our body and mind feel, the easier it is to deal with big emotions when they come up.

When you're feeling hungry, thirsty or didn't get enough sleep, are you more or less likely to get angry? Most of us get more grumpy and impatient at small things when we're not feeling our best… Rah certainly does!

No matter how well you look after your mind and body, things will still happen that hurt your feelings and you'll get angry – and that's OK. But when you're feeling your best, you have more energy and patience to deal with anger in a positive way.

EXCELLENT EXERCISE

We've already learned how brilliant moving your body is for calming big, angry feelings – but you don't need to save it just for those tricky moments! Exercising every day will help your body grow strong and healthy, and it also helps your mind relax.

When you exercise, your brain releases feel-good chemicals that lower stress and tension. When you wiggle, run and jump around, your troubles don't seem so bad.

Perhaps you love sport and you already have a favourite type of exercise. If sport isn't your thing, other brilliant forms of exercise include walking, playing outdoors and dancing.

ACTIVITY: BUST SOME MOVES!

When you dance, you can move your body however feels good! Dancing will make you smile and have fun. Why not put on some music and try out these moves:

Kick your legs

Wave your arms in the air

Run on the spot

Jump in the air

CHILLING OUT

Finding time to relax and do something quiet, fun and restful every day is really important. When you chill out, your body can re-energize and wind down from any stressful or annoying things that have happened to you that day.

Relaxing activities are things like:

- Reading a book

- Solving a puzzle

- Making art

- Colouring

- Gardening

- Playing quietly

- Doing yoga

Do you have any favourite relaxing activities? Write them here:

ACTIVITY: CHILL-OUT PLANNER

How will you relax each day this week? Plan your chill-out time using this planner:

Day	Chill-out time	Chill-out activity
Monday		
Tuesday		
Wednesday		
Thursday		
Friday		

ACTIVITY: MAKE A FIDGET STICK

If you're having a hard time with big feelings, having something to focus your attention on, like a fidget toy, really helps.

Scientists have found that moving your hands can help calm your whole body when you're feeling anger or anxiety.

You can make your own fidget toy with everyday craft materials – here's how:

You will need:

 Wooden lolly stick

 Sticky tape

 Pipe cleaner

 Scissors

 Small beads (big enough to fit the pipe cleaner through)

How to:

1. Bend the pipe cleaner around the lolly stick lengthways and trim any extra length.

2. Unbend the pipe cleaner and slide several beads on to it. You need to leave room for the beads to move up and down, so don't fill the pipe cleaner up with beads!

3. Use tape to fix the pipe cleaner to the lolly stick at both ends.

Carry your fidget stick around with you – you can use your fingers or thumbs to slide the beads up and down the pipe cleaner whenever you need to feel calm.

YUMMY, HEALTHY FOOD

Eating a good range of food is a big part of taking care of your body and mind. When you feed your body what it needs, you feel better able to cope with big feelings.

Listen to your body – it is very wise and will tell you when it's hungry and when it's had enough to eat!

ACTIVITY: CRUNCHY VEGGIE FINGERS

Crunchy foods help calm big emotions because they help you focus on three of your senses at once: taste, touch and sound.

Make a platter of crunchy veggie fingers to eat with your favourite dip. Simply ask a grown-up to help you cut some of the following vegetables into sticks:

Carrots

Celery

Cucumber

Bell peppers

TIME TO UNPLUG

Using a computer, tablet, phone or watching TV is fun, and there are loads of interesting and useful things the internet, films and TV shows can help us with. But screen time can also make us feel more impatient, more negative about ourselves and quicker to feel anger. That's why it's important to balance screen time with time away from screens.

What do you like to do that's screen-free?

Have you thought of trying out these ideas?

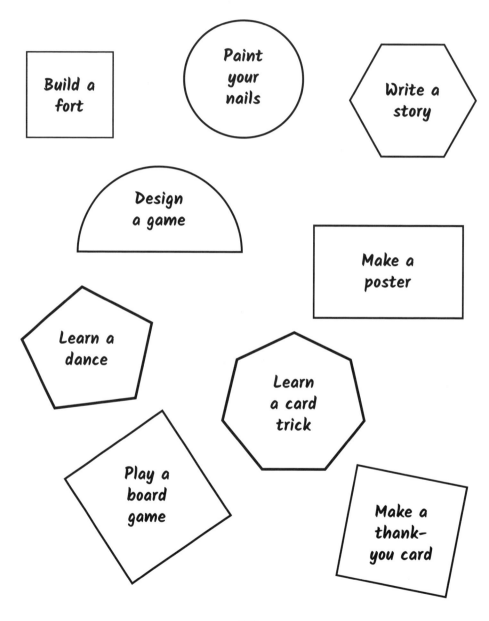

Build a fort

Paint your nails

Write a story

Design a game

Make a poster

Learn a dance

Learn a card trick

Play a board game

Make a thank-you card

GETTING PLENTY OF SLEEP

When you sleep, your mind and body can rest, grow and get ready for a new day. Dreams are your brain sorting through the things that happened during the daytime, making sense of them and calming your emotions. That's why, after something really annoys or upsets you, you often feel less angry about it the next day.

If you have trouble getting to sleep, try this breathing trick:

 Get cosy and lie in your bed with no distractions.

 Imagine you can breathe through the soles of your feet.

 As you breathe in, imagine pulling the air all the way through your body, from your feet right up and into your lungs.

 When you breathe out, imagine pushing the air all the way back down and out of the soles of your feet.

 Keep breathing like this, imagining your breath travelling up and down your body, until you're asleep.

Having a good night's sleep means you'll feel happier, more relaxed and better able to deal with big emotions the next day.

I LIKE MYSELF!

TAKING CARE OF YOUR MIND

Being kind to your mind is just as important as being kind to your body. When you take care of your mind, you're more resilient and you feel calm most of the time.

That's because when something happens that makes us feel an emotion, our brains make up a story about it, in the form of thoughts. Our thoughts make a difference to how we feel and behave. So, if your thoughts are positive, kind and generous to yourself and others, it's easier to feel calm.

It's Rah's birthday! Rah thought there would be lots of birthday cards delivered today, but it's time to go to school and none have arrived.

Rah's brain could come
up with all sorts of story
thoughts about this:

These story thoughts
lead to different
emotions:

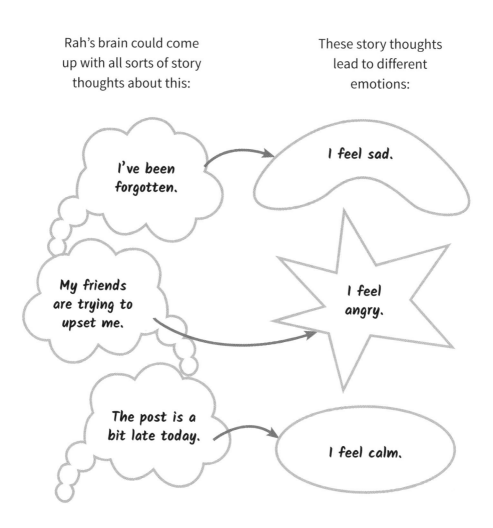

I've been
forgotten.

I feel sad.

My friends
are trying to
upset me.

I feel
angry.

The post is a
bit late today.

I feel calm.

It's not always easy to pick a different thought, especially if you're already feeling a big emotion. But remembering that different thoughts are possible and that these thoughts are not truths is the first step. The more you practise, the easier it will be.

ASKING FOR HELP

There are lots of things you can do to help calm big, angry feelings, but you don't have to do it alone. When you have friends and grown-ups who care about you, they can help you to calm angry feelings.

Asking for help can be tricky and it takes bravery – luckily, you're brave and you can do tricky things. Sometimes, writing a letter feels easier than talking. You could write something like this:

Dear...

When I feel angry I find it hard to calm my mind and body. Next time it happens, can you help me get calm?

I have a book with lots of ideas.

From,

Rah

I CAN DO
HARD THINGS

PART 6:
A BRIGHT FUTURE

It can be really frustrating when angry feelings hold you back from enjoying life. Learning skills to deal with angry feelings will make you more confident, calmer and a great friend. In this chapter we'll look at how you can use your new skills every day.

ACTIVITY: MY SMILE SHEET

It can be very hard to explain angry feelings to others, especially when you're feeling them! When you feel calm, make a smile sheet with some of the things you'd like the grown-ups in your life – your teachers, parents, carers and relatives – to know about you.

If it feels tricky, you can ask a trusted grown-up to help you fill it in.

> Think about what makes you a good friend, kind things that people have said about or to you, and what makes you special – e.g. creative, kind, funny.

> Think about the things that you think are important and the things that make you feel big, angry feelings – e.g. fairness/unfairness, honesty/ lying, being listened to/being ignored.

> Think about the tools you've learned about in this book and what helps big feelings move out of your body – e.g. belly breathing, a quiet place, using a fidget stick.

Name...

Age...

I'm brilliant because...

What's important to me...

You can help me calm big feelings with...

PUTTING THINGS RIGHT

Angry feelings can cause us to act and speak to people in ways we wouldn't when we feel calm. Sometimes this will happen. Making mistakes is part of being human, and the most important part is putting things right if we've hurt, frightened or upset someone because of our anger.

There are lots of ways to put things right! Here are a few ideas:

Saying "I'm sorry"

Asking "How can I help?"

Writing a letter

Offering a hug

Asking a grown-up to help me

Doing something kind

TALKING TO SOMEONE WHO HAS UPSET YOU

Often, angry feelings come up when something has happened that feels unfair or hurtful. Your feelings matter and it's OK to speak up for yourself. However, doing this when your mind and body are filled with anger usually ends up with the problem getting worse.

The best plan is to take a break to calm your mind and body, then – when you feel calm and ready – speak to the person who has upset you. It might be the case that they haven't done anything wrong, but your feelings are hurt. It's OK to express your feelings.

Here are some conversation starters for talking to someone who has upset you:

When you…	I felt…
Because…	I'd like it if…

ACTIVITY: COMPROMISE

You won't always get what you want. This can be tricky to handle and often brings up feelings of anger. Learning to calm your body and speak up for yourself will help you get *some* of what you want, which is called "compromise". Compromise means finding a solution to a problem that everyone feels OK with. It means no one gets exactly what they want, but no one gets none of what they want either.

For example, there are five cookies and two monsters. Both monsters want three cookies. A compromise is for both monsters to have two and a half cookies.

Now you try – help Rah find a compromise:

Rah wants to play catch and Chip wants to play basketball.

They could…

Play 10 minutes
of each game

Invent a new game
that mixes catch
and basketball

Play catch today and
basketball tomorrow

Find another ball and
play separately

Play a different
game instead

Keep arguing until it's
time to go home

Which compromise do you think is best? Draw a circle around it.

What made you pick this one?

I AM A
GOOD FRIEND

ACTIVITY: THINK IT THROUGH

Remember when we learned about taking a break on page 81? Taking a break allows you to calm your body, and it also allows you to calm your mind and think more clearly.

Thinking it through involves considering the consequences of any action you might take. So, for example, if Rah took Pip's smart new pencil case because Rah was feeling angry and jealous, a consequence might be that Pip is upset, doesn't trust Rah as much and Rah might get in trouble.

What are some consequences for these actions? Write your answers in the spaces below.

Action: It's time to go back to class, but Rah doesn't want to and throws a ball on the school roof.

Consequence: _____

_____

_____

_____

_____

Action: Chip didn't want a hug from Rah. Rah feels angry and pushes Chip over.

Consequence: _____

_____

_____

_____

_____

Action: Rah has been asked to help with the laundry. Rah would rather play video games and feels angry. Rah asks to take a break to calm down.

Consequence: _____

_____

_____

_____

_____

Your emotions, words and actions belong to you, and others' emotions, words and actions belong to them.

Although the angry feelings in your body and mind are yours to calm down, you can ask for help with this. You are not alone.

Emotions are tricky things and no one gets it right all the time. Learning to be aware of and find ways to deal with your feelings and actions will help you feel calmer, have more fun and be a great friend to yourself. You're doing really well and Rah is very proud of you.

You've got this!

DEALING WITH EMBARRASSMENT

You might feel embarrassed about something you did when you were feeling angry. It's OK – we all make mistakes. You become strong by learning from them and making a different choice next time.

Embarrassment is an emotion just like anger, sadness, happiness and worry. If you feel embarrassed, you can be kind to yourself and express it. Here are some ways to deal with feelings of embarrassment:

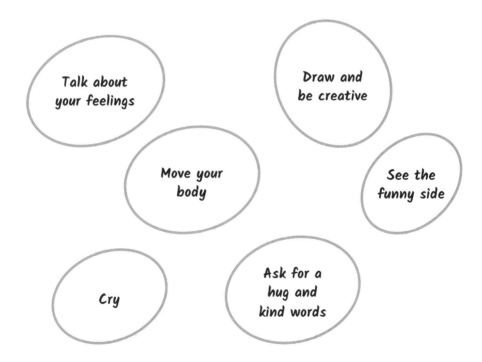

Talk about your feelings

Draw and be creative

Move your body

See the funny side

Cry

Ask for a hug and kind words

EMPATHY

When someone hurts our feelings and it makes us angry, it's easy to think the worst of them. Angry thoughts might sound like…

Empathy is the skill of seeing things from another point of view. When we take a moment to think things through, we can see that not everything that makes us feel angry is done on purpose, or with the intention of hurting our feelings.

Of course, it's still OK to feel angry… but using empathy to try to understand the other person will help calm those big, angry feelings.

Here's an example:

Rah's teacher asks the class to vote for this afternoon's activity: art or computer time.

Rah votes for art, but computing wins the vote.

Rah feels angry about this – Rah really wanted to do art! Rah thinks the teacher should have chosen art instead of doing a vote. Rah feels angry at the teacher and angry at the children who voted for computing.

Rah asks to take a break. Rah does some belly breathing (page 54) and thinks about a calm place (page 64). When Rah's body and brain feel calm enough, Rah can use empathy.

Rah's teacher comes to find Rah – now she uses empathy too!

When someone speaks to us with empathy, like Rah's teacher did, it helps us feel understood, which is an amazing way to calm angry feelings down.

ACTIVITY: MAKING CHANGES

Are there things you sometimes do, when you're feeling angry, that you'd like to change? Perhaps it's slamming doors or hitting? It's brave to decide to make a change for the better.

If you can think of something you do when you're angry, write it here:

What could you do instead? Think about the ideas in Part 4 or write your own:

What could help you? Think about the calming ideas in Part 3:

IT'S OK TO FEEL ANGRY

SHARING YOUR KNOWLEDGE

We're getting close to the end of the book – you've learned so much! You can use the things you've learned to help your friends, when there's a disagreement or angry feelings.

Here are some top tools for helping friends with angry feelings:

Remember: if someone nearby is angry and you feel scared or get hurt, it's important to move away from them. It's not your job to put yourself in harm's way to help with someone else's angry feelings.

ACTIVITY: MAKE YOUR OWN CALMING STATEMENTS

Create an eye-catching statement to put on your wall, mirror or fridge at home! Every time you see it, you'll feel a little calmer.

You will need:

 Coloured card

 Pencil

 PVA glue

 Fine paintbrush

 Eco-friendly glitter

 Old newspaper

How to:

1. Pick a positive statement that makes you feel calm, happy and in control. Flick back through this book to find ideas for positive statements!

2. Write it in big, neat letters on a piece of coloured card.

3. Use your paintbrush to carefully spread glue over the letters.

4. Sprinkle glitter over the glue and let it dry for about 30 seconds.

5. Tip the paper over some newspaper so all the leftover glitter slides off (you can then transfer the glitter back into its container).

6. Leave your calming statement to dry fully overnight.

GOLDEN RULES FOR WHEN I FEEL ANGRY

It's OK to feel angry

It's not OK to hurt others or damage things

Take a break when you feel angry

Be kind to yourself

Respect others

You can ask for help

INSPIRING STORIES

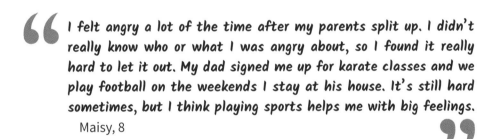

> I used to get really angry in class — it was so hard to sit still and I would end up ripping up my work that I'd spent lots of time on. My teacher helped me a lot — she said I can go into the corridor to take some deep breaths whenever I need to. Now I know I can do that, it's actually easier to stay calm at my desk. I still need to take a break sometimes though!

Luca, 10

> I felt angry a lot of the time after my parents split up. I didn't really know who or what I was angry about, so I found it really hard to let it out. My dad signed me up for karate classes and we play football on the weekends I stay at his house. It's still hard sometimes, but I think playing sports helps me with big feelings.

Maisy, 8

> My friend got a puppy and I felt so jealous and angry that I stole her backpack and threw it in a muddy puddle. Mum helped me write a letter to say sorry, and we washed her backpack together in the sink. Saying sorry is really hard — I'd rather wash a million backpacks! — but I'm glad I did it. After school I got to meet her puppy — he's soooo cute.

Mollie, 7

" Some other boys were calling me names and I really wanted to hurt them. Being disrespected makes me feel really angry. I was proud of myself though, I kept my cool, told them to back off and then went to play basketball with some mates instead. A bit of exercise really helps me calm myself down. "

Yusuf, 11

" There's this game I like on the computer right now, but sometimes the internet drops out and the game glitches. When that happens I get so angry. I got so frustrated the other day I ended up shouting at the computer. Mum came to see what was wrong and gave me a hug. She said she gets frustrated with computers, too, and together we worked out how to solve the problem. "

Edie, 9

THE END

You've reached the very end of the book. Rah's learned all about anger and calming big feelings – have you?

You can come back to this book any time you like – whether you need help calming down during a tough time, to help a friend understand anger or just to refresh your memory. You've worked really hard and should be very proud of yourself.

Don't forget: it's OK to feel angry!

YOU'VE GOT THIS!

For parents and carers: How to help your child deal with angry feelings

It's easy to think that we should keep our child's anger to a minimum, and discourage expressing it. Many of us were raised to associate our anger with being rude or behaving badly, and without guidance for expressing anger in healthy, productive ways.

Our children's anger can feel overwhelming and stressful to us as parents and carers. Even more so when it gets to a point where your child isn't able to control their behaviour. In these situations it's really important to calm yourself first – only when you're calm are you able to help your child navigate overwhelming emotions. This can be achieved by taking a couple of deep breaths, perhaps reminding yourself that you're safe, you can handle this and that your child is simply experiencing an emotion.

The bond you have with your child means your close, calm presence will help them find their own inner calm. When they're angry, it's a sign they need your help to make it through some big, difficult feelings. This can be hard to understand, especially when they're directing their anger at you and pushing you away. In these moments, they need to know that you are not afraid of their emotions. When they can see that you aren't afraid, they feel more confident in their own ability to cope.

Make sure that they're safe and let them be angry. Help them name their emotion and show that you understand (even if you feel they're overreacting or in the wrong): "You're feeling really angry, because…" When a child feels understood, this can diffuse and de-escalate a tense situation.

While a child – or a person of any age – is overwhelmed with anger, they aren't able to access the logical part of their brain, so it's best to save any discussion, concerns or consequences for once they're calm and can take your words on.

You can also model good anger management by letting your child hear you say out loud that you feel angry and what you are doing to calm yourself.

Your children learn so much from you, and seeing that it's normal to feel anger and take a break to calm down is very powerful.

I hope this book has been helpful for you and your child. Anger is such a difficult emotion to deal with, and you're doing a great job by helping your child gain knowledge and skills to express anger well and increase self-control.

Further advice

If you're worried about your child's mental health, or you think they need extra support with regulating their emotions, do talk it through with your doctor. While almost all children will struggle with angry feelings, some may need extra help. There are lots of great resources out there for information and guidance on children's mental health:

YoungMinds Parents' Helpline (UK)
www.youngminds.org.uk
0808 802 5544

BBC Bitesize (UK)
www.bbc.co.uk/bitesize/support

Childline (UK)
www.childline.org.uk
0800 1111

Child Mind Institute (USA)
www.childmind.org

The Youth Mental Health Project (USA)
www.ymhproject.org

Recommended reading

For children:
Anger Management Skills Workbook for Kids
Amanda Robinson

A Volcano in my Tummy
Éliane Whitehouse & Warwick Pudney

For adults:
The Whole-Brain Child
Dr Daniel J. Siegel and Dr Tina Payne Bryson

Calm Parents, Happy Kids: The Secrets of Stress-Free Parenting
Dr Laura Markham

Credits

Other books in the series...

Paperback
ISBN: 978-1-78783-699-0

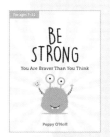

Paperback
ISBN: 978-1-78783-607-5

Paperback
ISBN: 978-1-78783-608-2

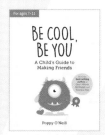

Paperback
ISBN: 978-1-80007-339-5

Paperback
ISBN: 978-1-78685-236-6

Paperback
ISBN: 978-1-78685-235-9

Paperback
ISBN: 978-1-80007-338-8

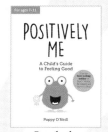

Paperback
ISBN: 978-1-80007-169-8

Paperback
ISBN: 978-1-80007-710-2

Paperback
ISBN: 978-1-80007-711-9

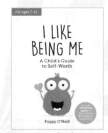

Paperback
ISBN: 978-1-80007-689-1

Paperback
ISBN: 978-1-80007-340-1

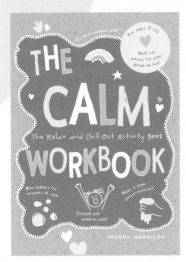

Paperback
ISBN: 978-1-80007-337-1

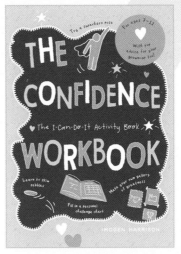

Paperback
ISBN: 978-1-80007-168-1

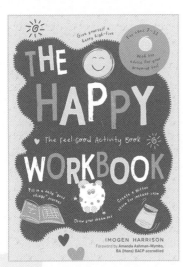

Paperback
ISBN: 978-1-78783-990-8

Paperback
ISBN: 978-1-78783-537-5

Have you enjoyed this book?
If so, why not write a review on your favourite website?

If you're interested in finding out more about our books, find us
on Facebook at **Summersdale Publishers,** on Twitter at **@Summersdale**
and on Instagram at **@summersdalebooks** and get in touch.
We'd love to hear from you!

Thanks very much for buying this Summersdale book.

www.summersdale.com